Douglas Johnson

Peruvian Daffodils, gouache on matboard, 7 3/8" x 5 1/2", 1994

Douglas Johnson

A Painter's Odyssey

Robert A. Ewing

Foreword by Stephen Parks

CLEAR LIGHT PUBLISHERS
SANTA FE

Clear Light Publishers, 823 Don Diego, Santa Fe, NM 87501
WEB: www.clearlightbooks.com

First Edition

10 9 8 7 6 5 4 3 2 1

Library of Congress Cataloging-in-Publication Data

Ewing, Robert A.

   Douglas Johnson: a painter's odyssey / Robert A. Ewing.

     p. cm

     ISBN 0-940666-91-X

     1. Johnson, Douglas, 1946-   —Criticism and interpretation.

   I. Title.

   ND237. J68E95   1997

   759.13—dc20   96-41850

                                              CIP

Printed and bound in Hong Kong, China by Book Art Inc., Toronto

Front Cover: *Still Life with Polychrome Pot, Kachina, Prayerstick and Mug*, gouache on matboard, 8$\frac{1}{2}$" x 6", 1995

Back Cover: *Mesa of Flowers*, gouache on paper, 6$\frac{1}{2}$" x 6$\frac{1}{2}$", 1991

Dedicated to my father, Herbert W. Johnson

ACKNOWLEDGMENTS

Robert L. Love

The Santa Fe Foundation

Herb Lotz, Photography

Sara Held

George H. Ewing

Marcia Keegan and Harmon Houghton

The Return Gallery Archives

Joseph I. Aragón

The Parks Gallery

The Gerald Peters Gallery

The Elaine Horwitch Gallery

Stuart Ashman

The Museum of New Mexico

Melissa Engstrom

Michael Motley

James DeVries

Nedra Matteucci's Fenn Galleries

Herbert Johnson

Sandra D'Emilio

Helen Doroshaw, Photography

Dan Morse, Photography

Lisbeth Loewenberg

Eleanor Morris Caponigro

Mary Rose

Sipapu, Place of Emergence, gouache on matboard, 5 7/8″ x 9″, 1995

Contents

Foreword

When people fall in love with northern New Mexico, they tend to fall hard, and suddenly. It happened to me in Taos in late September, 1973, on San Geronimo Day. On vacation from New York, I'd been camping in Colorado and decided to drive down for a brief visit. When I arrived the Indians were dancing at the Pueblo, dancing as they have for nearly a millennium. The expanse of landscapes running to the west left me breathless. The adobe buildings at the Pueblo and even in town were graceful and human-scaled. The sunset wouldn't quit— wave after wave of red roiling through the clouds. I was hooked, and twenty-three years later, I'm still hooked.

Falling in love with Douglas Johnson's paintings is a related phenomenon. We fall hard, and for many of the same reasons. I first saw his art in the late 1970s in what must have been the perfect setting, the Chaco-inspired, rock construction masterwork that was the Return Gallery in Taos. Johnson's tiny casein paintings hung like jewels on those immaculately fitted rock walls. They seemed miracles of color and detail, almost psychedelic in complexity and surreal juxtaposition, and yet so familiar! They were paintings of Anasazi and early pueblo culture—the pottery, the architecture, the costumes—aspects of which still surround us in northern New Mexico. Soon he was to add hallmarks of Hispanic life—and hallmarks of the region's natural life, the birds and flowers that flourish in the vicinity of his own rock home, built into a cliff some miles west of Abiquiú.

But it's the landscape that most defines the Southwest, and Johnson's paintings are usually anchored in it. Stretching out behind the ostensible subject of the painting is a horizon, and on it the artist often places one of the region's iconic landmarks, such as the Pedernal, the flat-topped monument of symmetry that dominates the skyline near his home, or the brooding presence of Black Mesa south of Española.

Not all of Johnson's paintings have been set in northern New Mexico. He's done series based on his travels in Mexico, South America, and the Far East, Thailand in particular. As exotic and alien as these settings seem, they are not much more exotic and alien than koshares at a San Ildefonso dance are to mainstream America, for example. They are compendiums of what the artist regards as the most beautiful and compelling aspects of a singular place.

The artist's ability to render the details of beauty is remarkable, and yet it doesn't begin to explain his greatness. Many others are as skilled at drawing, even on such a miniature scale. What I find most notable about Johnson's art is that these tiny paintings can be "read" and felt from such a great distance. At fifty feet I know I'm in the presence of one of his postcard-sized paintings.

Through some miracle of eye and art, I know these paintings long before I am able consciously to decode and appreciate their details. Colors call to me from across a very large room, announcing that his vision is present, alive, working on me long before I'm conscious of its contents.

The purity of the color must, at least in part, account for this art's ability to communicate over such relatively great distance; composition—the clean, faceted geometry of his paintings—must count, too. The artist's structured color has a crystalline gleam that excites the eyes, arouses interest, and draws the viewer in closer, into the details of this shimmering world of the ordinary transformed into the exotic.

These are not real colors of this region or any other, for that matter. The pueblo plazas are never so dustless and ordered as here. But as controlled and glorious as Douglas Johnson's vision is, it is not fantasy. He is accurately replicating his feelings about this place, its history, its people, what D. H. Lawrence called "the high-up quality of the day." Johnson's colors are the colors of our subjective experience of this oldest, most primal of the new worlds, New Mexico. They are the colors of our memories of it, the way we felt about the place when we discovered it a second ago or a year or a lifetime ago.

Douglas Johnson's paintings are about his love of this place. It sounds simplistic but I think it's true. They are about the details of his love and the pervasive qualities of it. They reveal his ecstatic connection with northern New Mexico and its indigenous peoples. They are labors of love, requiring intense concentration over days and weeks of effort, manifestations of a love that is glorious to behold.

STEPHEN PARKS

Snakes in the Grass, casein on paper, 10" x 16", 1973

CHAPTER ONE

The Early Years

Douglas Johnson's day begins with fire and water in rituals which have become commonplace by repetition. First he lights his stove with wood split the day before. He then carries two buckets of water up a steep path from a clear, cold spring nearby, first for morning coffee, next for cleansing body and habitation, and finally, and most importantly, for mixing the water-based gouache he uses to make his paintings. His paintings are an intrinsic part of his life.

In art we celebrate that which is unique, and individuals have often had to separate themselves from the mainstream in order to pursue a personal vision. A familiar example is found in the life of Georgia O'Keeffe, who left New York to live in New Mexico, where she found the solitude and inspiration she needed for her work. The flat-topped mountain called El Pedernal, so often a motif in O'Keeffe's work, can be seen from Douglas Johnson's land. He too has found solitude and inspiration in this extraordinary landscape; but beyond that he has integrated his life and art with the natural world around him. Within it he has created a private space that permits him to focus the energy he needs to create the intensely detailed, jewel-like works that have brought him acclaim far beyond the remote corner of New Mexico he has chosen for his own.

Much has been made of Johnson's reclusiveness. He has been called a hermit and a cave-dweller, but in actuality, he regularly participates in the world of gallery openings and art gatherings which form an integral part of the life of a successful artist. He is also an avid student of art, with an extensive personal library, and acknowledges influences as varied as Japanese art, traditional Navajo painting, and the work of European old masters, all of which resonate in his paintings. Douglas Johnson's life is truly an odyssey, beginning in the sometimes arid cultural environment of middle America in the 1950s and culminating in a life of richness and creativity far exceeding his boldest childhood dreams.

Douglas Walter Johnson was born on July 8, 1946 in Portland, Oregon. After his father, Herbert Johnson, was discharged from the Navy, he moved his family to the San Francisco Bay area, where he began working for Pan American Airlines in a job that required him to spend six months of each year on Wake Island in the Pacific, while Johnson's mother, Barbara, worked long hours to become successful selling real estate. A daughter, Claudia, was born in 1949.

With a father away for half of every year, and a mother increasingly involved with her work, Johnson was thrown on his own resources from an early age. He was a quiet, introspective child. Well-intentioned attempts to force him to be more outgoing and athletic only intensified his shyness.

The family lived for a while in Palo Alto, where Douglas began kindergarten in 1951. He remembers the keen pleasure he took in finger painting and other arts and crafts provided in his early school years. During the brief periods when his father was home from Wake Island, Johnson received attention and further encouragement in art. His father helped him with crayons and taught him how to draw subjects from the wartime South Pacific, such as airplanes and war ships, as well as familiar cartoon figures. He enjoyed the wonderful objects his father sent home from the Pacific, including large green glass balls used as fishnet floats, jagged pieces of white coral, and even a brass opium pipe, all packed in large wooden crates covered with exotic Japanese characters. His mother also enjoyed drawing and painting, and Johnson still has several of her drawings. It never occurred to anyone in his family, however, that art could be more than a pastime.

With a G.I. Bill loan, the Johnson family built a ranch style house in Los Altos in 1952. Johnson's mother helped design the house, which had wood-paneled interiors, knotty pine cabinetry, and hardwood floors. Watching the construction of the house from start to finish, he developed an interest in house construction at a very early age. The postwar building boom was in full swing at the time, and Johnson watched as hundreds of acres of orchard were leveled to make room for endless rows of ranch style homes. With the expansion of the real estate business, his mother became more involved in her work, while his father was increasingly committed to his distant work and travels. Eventually his parents divorced, and afterwards the children rarely saw their father. As their mother became busier with her work, she depended on her two children to help with household cooking and cleaning, and they had to fend for themselves much of the time.

In the second grade Johnson was given the then popular paint-by-numbers sets, but instead of painting the number compositions, he opened the capsules of oil paint, experimented with them, and created his own paintings. The following year, his teacher introduced him to subjects that galvanized his imagination and that continue to figure prominently in Johnson's art today. Miss Hamilton, who had taught in the Southwest and had traveled to Egypt, gave her class mimeographed images of Indians and scenes from Egypt to color. Johnson's meticulous work with these drawings and his imaginative color combinations brought

Douglas and his sister, Claudia, Los Altos, California, circa 1954

him his first recognition: he was pronounced the best artist in the class. At a time when athletics were the approved activities for young boys, it was an important revelation to find encouragement and approval for an activity that he loved and in which he excelled.

In 1957 Barbara Johnson remarried and the family settled in the town of Twain-Harte in the Sierra Nevadas, and a half brother, Mark, was born. An important memory of that time was seeing the film *The Ten Commandments*, an overwhelming experience of color and spectacle that stimulated Johnson's interest in ancient cultures. This interest was furthered indirectly by his stepfather, Frank Hall, who was an avid reader. He taught Johnson the value of books and encouraged him to check books out of the public library. Most of the books he chose dealt with the topic of ancient

Pecos Church, 1680, gouache on matboard, 7" x 8 3/4", 1996

Southern Pacific Train near Bakersfield, California. An early photo by
Douglas Johnson photographed at age 15

Rods and Wheels, pencil on paper, 11 1/2" x 16 1/2", 1962

history, and from these books Johnson developed a lasting interest in art history and archaeology.

Frank Hall lost a series of jobs during this period because of alcoholism, and the family was uprooted once again. Unemployed and without money, Hall was forced to move the family to his mother's home in Pacific Grove, California.

Under the guidance of their step-grandmother, the children attended the historic church at the old Carmel Mission and were baptized as Catholics in a baptismal font in which Father Junipero Serra had baptized thousands of Indians. This was Johnson's first experience with spirituality, and he became very serious about his new religion. He received the sacraments and was confirmed in the Church. He also read the Catholic bible omnivorously, reveling in its historical descriptions. Johnson faithfully attended church until his first year of college, when he found other avenues to express his personal spiritual needs. It was also at this time that the ritual of the mass underwent changes. The altar was turned toward the congregation and the mass was simplified and translated into English. The atmosphere of mysticism that had inspired Johnson had disappeared from the ritual.

After a brief period in Pacific Grove, Johnson finished the sixth grade, receiving an award for having completed the most book reports in class, all of which were on the topic of ancient history and illustrated with his own drawings of Greek, Egyptian, or Mayan architecture.

Moving from place to place, and from school to school became a way of life for the family. With little time to develop friendships, Johnson spent most of his time alone, reading or drawing, living in imaginary worlds from other times. He was very close to his sister Claudia, and in their play they acted out ancient history, portraying such characters as Antony and Cleopatra.

In search of employment, Frank Hall next moved the family to Bakersfield, California, where he found work as an oil truck driver. The Santa Fe Railroad in Bakersfield was filled with bustling activity. Long freight trains continually arrived and departed, traveling back and forth from the Southwest. The railyard, which was a short bicycle trip from Johnson's home, became a haven on weekends and holidays during a period when life at home was deteriorating because of his stepfather's drinking. More than an escape from a painful situation, the railroad fed a great fascination with trains and travel that had come to fill Johnson's world and find expression in his art.

During that year he was encouraged by an art teacher, Miss Irene Dennin, who predicted that he would become an artist and gave him special attention after school. Johnson had begun painting trains, and at the teacher's urging, he entered one of his paintings in a local art show and won a second prize ribbon. He was introduced to tempera paint on rough watercolor paper as a medium, and although he experimented with other media in school, it was primarily tempera and other water-based media such as casein and gouache that he continued to work in throughout the following decades.

Photographs of the family at this time showed them living in a typical 1950s home with bare walls, blond Danish modern furniture, a chrome and Formica dining room set, and plastic "Melmac" dishes; but Johnson's bedroom was a private world of his own creation. A four- by eight-foot board held a model train set that became a focus for his developing art and provided his first opportunity to create scaled-down landscapes, which remain prominent in his work today. For the train set he created a miniature southwestern landscape through which tiny Santa Fe trains ran on timetables he had meticulously hand-painted. It was a safe, self-contained world. Johnson himself believes his compulsion to create order and harmony began as a response to the chaos of his family's life during this period. He experienced a terrifying fever dream during a childhood illness in which he recalls, "I saw chaos all about me. Rooms were disheveled, everything broken and floating in space. It was so frightening I've tried since then to put the pieces back together, arrange them in beauteous order."

Johnson filled his bedroom with the images that possessed his imagination. He collected all kinds of artifacts carrying the Santa Fe railroad logo. The walls of the room were decorated from floor to ceiling with posters and magazine cutouts of Santa Fe trains, southwestern landscapes with mesas and canyons, Indian pueblos, and Spanish villages. These would remain recurrent motifs in his mature work.

When his father sent him a new thirty-five millimeter camera from Japan for Christmas, another artistic dimension opened. Johnson began experimenting with composition in a rectangular format and took hundreds of pictures of trains entering and leaving Bakersfield. The great silver streamlined trains truly fascinated him, with their fanciful Indian names and gleaming, powerful locomotives painted like Indian chiefs. They pulled into the station carrying prosperous looking people in luxurious coaches, dining cars, and Pullman sleepers and departed to the exotic southwestern destinations that increasingly dominated his imagination.

In 1961 Johnson entered Bakersfield High School, which was next to the Santa Fe railyard. The sound of trains created a background for his art classes, where he continued to create visual fantasies of deserts, Indian people, adobe architecture, and Santa Fe trains.

In 1962 his mother divorced Frank Hall and moved to Portland, Oregon, where his maternal grandmother lived. When his mother, younger brother, and sister returned to Los Altos, Johnson remained in Portland to attend summer school.

He continued photographing trains at Union Station, terminus of several of the most colorful and magnificent passenger trains of the period. He rejoined the family in the fall and began his sophomore year at Los Altos High School, while his mother returned to the all-consuming real estate business.

Johnson's paintings from this period are quite remarkable for a high school student. They have an inventive sense of composition combined with a mastery of detail that remains characteristic of his later work. He sold a pencil drawing executed in a design class to a friend of his mother's, who displayed it in a downtown title company office (see page 14). He could see it through the window every time he rode his bicycle downtown. Though the sale was encouraging, and he had his first "one-man show" in a school showcase during his senior year, Johnson still did not consider art as a potential means of making a living. That year he took courses in industrial design, architectural drawing, and drafting, which would be the only formal art training he ever received.

Johnson entered San Jose State College in 1964, intending to major in psychology. There he discovered the work of Salvador Dalí and the Surrealists, which became a major influence in his painting. Living away from home for the first time, he began hitching rides on freight trains on weekends, in an exciting and often frightening pursuit of his obsession with trains. After reading Jack Kerouac's *On the Road*, he and a friend decided to ride freights to New Orleans during spring break at the college. Although the trip was never completed, it became a turning point in his life. On a freight heading east from West Texas, his friend was riding with his feet hanging outside a boxcar door and on a narrow bridge hit them on a railing, breaking several bones. It wasn't until the train reached Fort Worth that Johnson was able to get help for his friend.

16

Douglas Johnson, age 17, Los Altos, California

Leaving him in a hospital, Johnson returned home via a more northerly route, eventually connecting with the Santa Fe railroad at Amarillo.

Crossing New Mexico and Arizona in the following days, Johnson saw for the first time the grandeur of the southwestern landscape, realizing his long-cherished dream. He remembers traveling through central New Mexico speeding by cliffs and hillsides blazing in the sunset. The freight train he was riding passed a Super Chief speeding in the opposite direction bathed in vivid golden light. He saw the Laguna Pueblo and the farming villages of Ácoma, whose golden stone walls reminded him of ancient mythical cities. The next day the train passed through a fresh snowfall near Flagstaff, Arizona. Johnson, deeply touched, knew his life had been irrevocably changed. He returned to California alone and penniless, but he had seen for himself the deserts, the Indians, and the landscapes of the Southwest, and he knew that everything he had dreamed of actually existed.

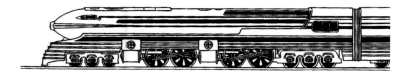

1956 Oldsmobile, gouache on matboard, 7″ x 5 1/2″, 1994

Cruisin' To Santuario, gouache on paper, 5 7/8" x 7 3/4", 1988

Mandala, Shiprock to Mesa Verde, casein on paper, 25"x 25", 1972

CHAPTER TWO

Navajo Country: The Awakening

Back in school, Johnson was restless for further adventure and hungry to return to the Southwest, which he had glimpsed so briefly. A recruiter convinced him to join the Vista program, a domestic Peace Corps that was part of President Johnson's war on poverty. After six intensive weeks of training in Indian culture and self-awareness at the University of Utah in Salt Lake City, he requested to be assigned to Chinle, Arizona, in the heart of the Navajo Reservation. His new home was a world of horizontal mesas and vast open spaces cut with deep red sandstone canyons, the ever-changing skies filled with towering summer thunderheads.

Douglas Johnson's first job was to help establish a preschool that opened with some thirty Navajo students in the fall of 1965. The children, who were around five years old, came in from the surrounding desert with no knowledge of English and had never been away from their families or hogans. They were silent and terrified. Working with a bilingual Navajo teacher and two Navajo aides, he helped teach rudimentary English, as well as how to eat with spoons and forks, and how to use bathroom facilities, introducing the students to what was literally a foreign culture. Johnson began learning the Navajo language from the teachers and students and later from Navajo friends. He became as much a student of their culture as they were of his. A textbook published by the Bureau of Indian Affairs entitled *The Little Herder*, beautifully illustrated by Hoke Denetsosie with stylized line drawings of Navajo life in the 1930s, so inspired Johnson that he copied many of the drawings in his spare time. They were representative of the style that had been taught to Indian art students by Dorothy Dunn at the Santa Fe Indian School during the 1930s and 1940s. Her students were encouraged to portray their traditional culture in a simple, delicate, linear style similar to that of ancient pottery design and kiva mural painting. It was a style that lent itself to Johnson's hard-edged drafting and drawing techniques.

Johnson found friends among the Navajo who were like him, gentle and introspective; yet they were fearless in the hard business of surviving in a difficult land—a place where raising sheep, farming, weaving, and jewelry making were the main ways to make a living. He became friends with a Navajo his own age, David Wilson, who lived at Canyon del Muerto. David's family, like other Navajo, had been given "American" names by the traders at Chinle. David Wilson and his younger brothers became like a family to Johnson. When not involved in his Vista duties, he spent time with the Wilsons, walking the ancient trails from the canyon rim to the summer hogan in the depths of the canyon. He planted corn, squash, and beans with the Wilson boys, using a horse-drawn plow. The Wilson women prepared seed near the hogan, then often butchered a goat to feed the men at midday. Johnson says that the smell of roasting goat ribs over an open fire with fry bread and boiled coffee still vividly evokes memories of that period. While in the canyon, Johnson and the Wilson boys explored the great Anasazi cliff ruins that filled nearly every cave in the vicinity. Mummy Cave Ruin, a small cliff city, was the

The hogan on the rim of Canyon del Muerto where Johnson lived in 1966-1967

Douglas Johnson with his pottery, 1974

most impressive with its high square tower and many tiny rooms filled with painted potsherds, old yucca sandals, and weaving and basketry fragments. In one kiva painted murals were still visible.

Johnson remembers walking across the canyon to the sheep camp in the Black Rock area in the company of Tsebinascloni, father and grandfather of the family. Isolated and reachable only by foot or on horseback, the camp was a world of dense piñon forests with hogans at the end of winding foot trails. Johnson spent many days with the elder Wilson in this area and was later joined by the rest of the family, who brought provisions on horseback along with their herd of sheep and goats. The way of life there had changed little in modern times. Mutton, potatoes, tortillas, and wild herbs were the basic foods. To obtain water the old man would dig a hole in a dry arroyo, which filled from a hidden spring. Johnson slept with the family on the male side of the hogan on sheepskins under soft wool Pendleton blankets.

He eventually moved into an abandoned hogan owned by the Wilson family on the canyon rim. Living in the hogan without utilities or creature comforts prepared him for the way of life he would choose in later years. Discovering that he could survive without modern amenities, he became accustomed to carrying his daily water and using wood fires for heating and cooking.

For the remainder of his two-year Vista enlistment Johnson and two other Vista volunteers, Tessa Stanwood and Tina Willis, established a local newspaper, *Diné Bizaad*, for the Chinle community. The paper, which Johnson edited, gave the Navajos a voice in the otherwise government-controlled community, printing not only traditional Navajo stories and myths, but becoming a vehicle for protest.

As Johnson's interest in Southwest Indian culture and art deepened, he began to study old Anasazi and modern

Hopi pottery as well as the Navajo rug designs still woven in every hogan during that period. Also exposed to the rich oral tradition of the Navajo people, Johnson had the opportunity to hear Navajo stories describing the disappearance of the Anasazi, the Ute invasions, the arrival of the Spanish and Americans, and the exile and the Long Walk to Bosque Redondo.

Prints of the paintings of Harrison Begay were displayed and sold everywhere on the reservation. They were influenced by Dorothy Dunn, strong in design, delicate in brushwork, with soft pastel desert colors and possessing a powerful spiritual content. Johnson paraphrased these paintings with his own temperas on colored mat board. The Begay prints depicted a classic Navajo world devoid of contemporary motifs. Johnson describes it as

a poetic world of beauteous horses ridden by traditionally dressed Navajos, adorned with turquoise and silver, with their hair flawlessly dressed. The sheep were fat, the people beautiful and lean, the land bountiful. It was a world I saw rapidly changing, sadly falling apart, preserved by Begay as if it were a dream from which the Navajo were beginning to awake.

Johnson attended many dances and ceremonials, particularly the nighttime Yei Bi Chai and Fire dances. He observed "sings," healing rites performed over the sick by medicine men or women utilizing chants and elaborate sand paintings, ritual objects, and body painting. He sat on the male side of the hogan, holding rattles, and learned to chant. Much of this experience would find its way into his painting in the future, especially the Yei figures in the sand paintings, and the face and body painting. He also experimented with peyote and remembers seeing hallucinatory images in the firelight, many of which were to manifest later in his art.

Cliffhouse, Canyon del Muerto, gouache on paper, 5 7/8" x 3 3/8", 1979

23

The Pink Pueblo, gouache on paper, 6 3/8″ x 9 1/8″, 1981

Recently, when asked to write about his perceptions and experience of the Navajo way of life, Johnson began by discussing sandpainting and its relation to the art, world view, and religions of Asia, from where, it is believed, the ancestors of the Navajo migrated.

Sandpainting is the most ancient and evolved expression of this art. A sandpainting is an instrument of healing. It is an illustration in colored sands of a myth, a story of the Yei or gods. It is a mandala created on a hogan floor, almost the size of the hogan, in the shape of a circle, all colors evoking meaning. The person to receive healing sits at its center and through elaborate ritual becomes part of the myth, and walks among the Yei. The "patient" leaves the mandala healed and in harmony with nature at the ceremonial's conclusion. Then the entire sandpainting is destroyed, its sands buried or scattered to the winds. Buddhists today also create sandpaintings in the form of mandalas and they too are destroyed after creation. This is ritual art created solely for the purpose of ceremony.

Navajos also believe themselves to be selfless as in the Buddhist way. The individual does not exist in a western European sense. A Navajo exists as part of his family, his clan, his people. He shuns competition. He strives to equal his fellow man, never to stand above him. A Navajo's life traditionally was sparse and simple; he never possessed more than he needed, giving away his excess. He lived with others in a simple one room dwelling, the round hogan, and observed nature in an awesome landscape with respect, taking only what he needed. He was able to stand alone, in a seemingly endless desert expanse, secure and content. For the Navajo all of nature was animated in his myths in a belief that all elements of nature were alive with spirit. A rock could speak, clouds were a tribe of "cloud people," animals and plants were the equals of humans. Of course the effects of the European invasion have eroded many traditional Navajo beliefs.

Observing Navajo women at their looms in windowless hogans, sometimes working into the night by firelight, was inspirational to my own manner of creating art. These women became immersed in their weaving—it was a form of meditation. Slowly a textile would emerge on an upright loom, sometimes dwarfing its creator, bold in its geometric design and native colors, purely Navajo. I modeled my easel and painting technique after this image. I too am content with a simple life, living in the rich grandeur of an animate landscape.

Working in the Vista program became more and more difficult for Johnson, since by this time it seemed to him that the Navajo had more to teach him than he had to teach them. Years later when looking back upon the Vista program and the lives of the volunteers, he believes that the volunteers who went to the Indian reservations were changed by the Indians much more than they changed the lives of the Indians. "We were all too young to offer anything of value to the Indians," Johnson recently wrote. "We were of an unhappy generation in search of meaning for our own lives. Our culture and religion had let us down, failed us, and we were desperate for new meaning, ripe for new interpretations of life." Johnson's decision to become an artist was influenced by seeing that the Navajo could make a living through their craft and art. He also knew by this time that he did not want to return to his own culture and the kind of life it offered, which had no meaning for him. While living among the Navajo, he acquired a sense of direction, both personally and creatively, that remains alive within him. Years later he could still say, "My whole viewpoint today is based on the Navajo idea of harmony. Not only with nature, but also with other people and within your own body."[1]

When his Vista term ended in the summer of 1967, Johnson returned to San Francisco with a treasure of Indian artifacts, rugs, pottery, and jewelry. He tried to recreate a hogan in a Victorian apartment in the Haight-Ashbury district of the city. Working for a record distribution company, he tried to become part of life in San Francisco, then at the height of the hippie free-love, peace, and drug culture.

26

Reaching for the Sky, gouache on paper, 10 5/8" x 8 1/8", 1978

Chickens, gouache on matboard, 5 3/4" x 8 1/2", 1995

The Haight-Ashbury, tempera on paper, 11" x 8", 1967

Many hippies in Haight-Ashbury were trying to create their vision of Indian life in an urban center. Johnson, who had experienced the real thing, was again isolated. So little was known about actual Indian life at that time that few of his true-life stories of the Navajo were believed. He found the hippies to be interested primarily in the trappings—feathers, beads, peyote, and whatever mysterious herbs were smoked in "peace-pipes."

On his own time Johnson continued producing small tempera paintings of Indian subjects as well as surreal images of buildings in San Francisco and, as always, trains. The paintings were intricately designed and, compared to his work today, executed in very muted colors. As always, the compositions were strong, and the work was characterized by careful detail. Few people were attracted to his work since it did not conform to the abstract styles popular at the time. He found that galleries were not interested in representational work. He tried involving himself with what remained of the "Beat" movement in San Francisco, but didn't feel comfortable with the Beatniks' preoccupation with alcohol, abstraction in art, and nihilistic philosophy.

For a time, he was employed in a bookstore owned by a man named Bruno Loewenberg, who became a major influence in his life. Loewenberg, an elderly Jewish man, had survived the holocaust in Nazi Germany when he was bought out of Buchenwald. He made his way to San Francisco, via Israel and Shanghai, by buying and selling used books. He had known many of the German Expressionists and introduced Johnson to the works of Nolde, Beckman, and George Grosz as well as the French Impressionists. Although he was critical of Johnson's paintings, he was fond of him and let him have a small show in the bookstore on Polk Street. One painting sold for sixty dollars. It was in this bookstore that Johnson, under the tutelage of Loewenberg, began a lifelong study of art history from books.

In 1968, Johnson made a journey to Boston to visit friends. He painted for several weeks in Provincetown, a town with an active art colony on the tip of Cape Cod. He hitchhiked up and down the Cape painting lighthouses and white, shuttered New England style cottages. Reflecting the influence of the surrealist painter Magritte, he also painted giant seashells or crabs on tiny docks against the dark blue Atlantic Ocean. He carried all his possessions on his back, including his paints and brushes, with his large drawing pad full of finished paintings under his arm. Renting small rooms at night, he painted on the floor. Although filled with his usual careful detail and appropriately Atlantic coastal color, the paintings did not find an audience. It was not the way people painted at the time, but Johnson continued to develop his own style regardless of public opinion.

Johnson returned from the Boston area by train—transcontinental streamliner, The Canadian—traveling from Montreal to Vancouver, savoring the long train trip across Canada. He headed south on the West Coast, visiting relatives in Portland, and eventually arriving in San Francisco. Feeling increasingly alien there, he was impelled to return to the Navajo Reservation.

Johnson could see that his work was improving, and he continued to believe that it would eventually find an audience. After managing to sell several paintings to friends, he raised enough money to return to Chinle in the summer of 1969. Committed to devoting all his energies to painting, he returned to the reservation with his paints and paper, a collection of art books, and a few necessities. He took up residence with seventy-year-old Tahcheeni Yazzie at the foot of Black Mountain.

Yazzie was the mother of Sybil Yazzie-Baldwin, Johnson's former associate teacher at the pre-school in Chinle, who had studied with Dorothy Dunn at the Santa Fe Indian

School. A traditional Navajo, Tahcheeni always dressed in the native costume of long flowing skirts and velveteen blouse decorated with myriad silver buttons. She wore wonderful silver and turquoise bracelets and ancient turquoise beads. She herded sheep every day, chopped her own wood for cooking, and wove blankets at night by the light of a kerosene lamp. Johnson helped herd her sheep in return for meals and the use of an empty hogan in her sheep camp.

The landscape here was different from the canyon country, open and expansive with occasional red sandstone monoliths. Black Mountain was a dark, mysterious eroded wall rising above the plain. Beyond the mountain was the last untouched frontier of the Navajo, a land that stimulated Johnson's imagination. Here the ruins of the Anasazi stood untouched, and Indians still walked ancient trails and traveled on horseback.

He spent his evenings around the fire with Tahcheeni and other Navajos who gathered to chew piñon nuts and tell stories. By this time he could understand Navajo, and he committed to memory the stories he heard about the creation of the Navajo world, along with the deeds of the Warrior Twins and the powers of the Holy People depicted in sand paintings.

During this time a daughter of Tahcheeni taught Johnson the rudiments of pottery making. She took him to a clay dig at the foot of Black Mountain and demonstrated how to find clay by tasting it and dissolving it in the mouth to test the texture and consistency. She taught him how to coil pots with ropes of wet clay, how to apply red clay mixed to the consistency of cream called slip, and polish the pot with smooth basalt polishing stones. When they had dried, she took Johnson's first pots to a waterhole where cows had left behind an ample supply of dried manure. They started a fire with cedar bark and covered the pots with manure. After

Ceremonial Chamber, gouache on paper, 7 3/4" x 5 1/2", 1977

Shucked Corn, gouache on paper, 5 3/4" x 8 3/4", 1982

many hours the pots emerged with beautiful smoke clouds on their surfaces.

He has continued to make pottery in this way throughout his career, although under the tutelage of pueblo potters his pots have become much more sophisticated. Many years later, when he took Tahcheeni one of his mature pots, a highly polished redware bowl with painted black designs, she would not believe he had made it, thinking he had taken it from an Anasazi ruin or burial.

By the time winter approached, Johnson had completed many paintings. The light, so generous in summer, dimmed, and with the door closed against the approaching cold, the hogan became dark. The smoke hole in the ceiling did not admit enough light by which to paint.

NOTES

1. Kathryn Colmer, "Revitalizing Ritual," *Southwest Art*, June 1987, 44.

Revolt, after Fred Kabotie, gouache on paper, 10 3/8" x 7 1/8", 1981

Bull Rushes with Harvest Moon, gouache on paper, 6 5/8" x 8 7/8", 1986

Ruins of the Old Palace Hotel, Cerrillos, N.M., casein on paper, 5″ x 8 1/2″, 1972

CHAPTER THREE

Aztlán, Land of Enchantment

In October 1969, Douglas Johnson accompanied the Yazzie-Baldwin family to visit their son at St. Catherine's Indian School in Santa Fe. It was his first visit to the city that was the namesake of the railroad that had entranced him from childhood. Although Johnson had long been fascinated with Santa Fe, the actuality surpassed even his imagination. This was Aztlán, the legendary site of Aztec emergence, and the homeland of the Pueblo Indians, ancient and modern. It had roots in both the Spanish quest for cities of gold and centuries of Spanish settlement in an isolated frontier. Surrounded by piñon- and juniper-studded hills and the majestic Sangre de Cristo Mountains, Santa Fe had long been a center for the arts. Built around a central plaza dominated by the centuries-old Palace of the Governors, now a historical museum, and the impressive adobe style Fine Arts Museum, Santa Fe was a place where the arts mattered. Johnson felt that here his work would be understood.

To Johnson it seemed destined that he would find himself in the town for which the Santa Fe Railroad was named, and he determined to move to the area as soon as possible. While buying art supplies, he met an artist named John Wagner, who introduced him to Cerrillos, a small community south of Santa Fe where a number of young artists lived and worked. Johnson returned to the reservation for Thanksgiving and moved to Cerrillos soon after.

Johnson refers to his years in Cerrillos as the "Van Gogh period" in his life. While there was a certain romance in living the life of a starving artist, he existed in real poverty and was often hungry. He had rented a tiny house in Cer-

rillos for twenty dollars a month and managed to eke out an existence on fifteen dollars a week for the rest of his needs. Once a week he hitched a ride to Santa Fe to buy art supplies and provisions and wash his clothes at a laundromat. In Cerrillos he was surrounded by a group of vital, emerging young artists, who inspired and encouraged one another.

The Cerrillos house had electricity and cold water that only began to run once the pipes thawed in the spring. A poorly built fireplace in one corner gave out some heat. Every day Johnson cut firewood and carried it in big bundles on his back to the fireplace, which had become his closest friend. He painted sitting on the floor in front of it and slept on a Navajo style bed near its warmth.

Little by little Johnson began to gain recognition, showing his work first at Painter's Gallery on Canyon Road in Santa Fe, where he made his first sale in January 1970. In the spring he opened the little house in Cerrillos on weekends, calling it Salt Gallery, after a prominent Navajo clan. He planted a large vegetable garden in the yard between his back door and the Santa Fe Railroad tracks, which passed nearby. Johnson made his own eating utensils of clay and fired them in the fireplace. Life was difficult, but he found it very fulfilling. The Navajos had given him the tools for survival, and his few sales kept him alive until the spring of 1970, when the Santa Fe Art Community began to become aware of Johnson and his unique paintings.

If Johnson's life was limited by economics, it was expanding rapidly in other ways. He began attending the openings of exhibitions at art galleries and museums and

Prayerstick, mixed media, 16" x 3", 1986

became interested in the work of early Taos and Santa Fe artists such as Blumenshein, Phillips, Sharp, Couse, and Gustave Baumann. He freely admits to having been part of the drug culture of the time, which certainly influenced the extraordinarily detailed mandalas, filled with Indian symbolism, that he was painting. He began attending the extraordinary ceremonials of the Pueblo Indians, which became a major source of inspiration, as they are in his life and in his work to this day.

For many years, Indians from Santo Domingo Pueblo had been coming to Cerrillos to sell jewelry, pottery, and vegetables from their fields. Among the people Douglas met were Lupe and Juan Montoya, who became fascinated by his lifestyle and art, especially his polished redware pottery. Lupe was a potter, but could no longer see well enough to paint her pots. She invited Johnson to her house in the pueblo, set him up with her slips and paints in a back room, and taught him how to paint her pottery. In exchange for this service she fed him well and taught him the techniques of polychrome pottery making. Johnson became a friend of her family and renewed his sense of kinship with Native Americans and their way of life.

In 1970, while I was director of the Museum of Fine Arts in Santa Fe (a division of the Museum of New Mexico), I was challenged by a group of young artists—including Johnson—to present an exhibition of their work. While their individual styles ranged from careful realism to complete abstraction, they asked to be exhibited together because all of their work reflected their commitment to living and working in New Mexico. As director, I found them and their work stimulating and provocative, and the exhibit that resulted, titled "Eight from Santa Fe," was something of a sensation. Of the eight, Douglas Johnson, Dennis Culver, and Sam Scott remain active and important members of the Santa Fe arts community. In the catalogue for the exhibit I wrote:

Johnson at age 27, Agua Sarca, 1974

The eight young artists represented here are as individual as artists have always been and do not want to be thought of as a group beyond this exhibition. Collectively, their lifestyles link them with the colorful generation which enlivens our world and defies categorization. They speak rationally of the illogical—and logically of the irrational. Their work ranges from pure abstraction to mystic realism executed in whatever materials are relevant to their needs.

The perspective of time will be needed before posterity can decide which artists most accurately represent this time and point the way to the future. . . . For now this exhibition provides an opportunity to participate in the exciting and joyful thing it is to be alive in the 1970s in Santa Fe.[1]

Asked to contribute a statement to the catalogue, Douglas Johnson wrote:

I am a landscape painter. My mandala paintings are landscapes. They attempt to express the harmonious composition of nature. My use of color is influenced by the fine, herbal dyed yarns of Navajo weaving. With line and pattern I attempt to create rhythm and vibration. I try to paint the earth vibrant and changing with the seasons, softly imprinted with the passing of the Indian people, and the sky active and forever sweeping the land with sculpturing wind and water. I paint the marriage between Father. Sky and Mother Earth, and of their children and of their lives.[2]

Art critic Virginia Kirby, writing about Douglas Johnson's paintings in the exhibition, was among the first commentators to see the unique vision in his work. She wrote:

Douglas Johnson explores space-time relationships in a highly individual way. He seems to search for the exact point of intersection between the inner and outer landscapes. The paintings seem to accomplish a sort of time-stop. Landscapes are trapped and held still. Form is both broken and restored.[3]

Recognition came steadily as a few art collectors in

Arranging finished pots and tiles on grill before firing

Fired pottery bowls

Recently fired pots still in the ashes

Pots drying, waiting to be fired

Santa Fe made the journey to Cerrillos to acquire Johnson's paintings, and he was able to trade thirteen of his San Francisco paintings for land in Cerrillos. After visiting the great Anasazi ruins at Chaco Canyon, with its elegant stone masonry, he built a stone house on his land. The first house he had ever owned, it consisted of just one room in which he painted, ate, and slept. It had unique features such as a bed that could be raised to give access to the kitchen beneath the floor level.

He sought out people, many of them Pueblo Indians, who shared his personal values and who felt and lived in kinship with the land. For a time he made extra money buying and selling Indian art, as had the early Taos and Santa Fe artists. Welcoming design challenges, he became a self-taught architect, as well as a pottery maker and print-maker. He decorated his pottery with designs that developed from his mandala painting style.

As his own fortunes ascended, those of other members of his family went into decline. He learned that his sister Claudia had been irretrievably caught up in the then little-understood disorder called anorexia, and his mother had developed serious alcoholism. On the positive side, he had been reunited with his father, who journeyed to Cerrillos in 1970 to visit the son of whom he had become very proud.

In 1972, several art galleries in Santa Fe were interested in Johnson's work, including the Jamison Gallery, which was one of the most important in town. The gallery was originally organized by Bland Jamison, a long-time Santa Fe resident who had been preparing to open a gallery for several years. He died unexpectedly just before it was to open, but Margaret Jamison, his widow, managed to open the gallery on schedule. It turned out that Margaret Jamison not only had an excellent eye for art, she also was to become one of the first gallery owners in Santa Fe to show contemporary works on a regular basis. She provided a

Awaiting the Emergence into The Fifth World, 22 x 15, casein on paper, 1970

crucial boost to the establishment of Santa Fe as a center of contemporary art and encouraged and supported the careers of a whole new generation of artists who would contribute to the development of southwestern art.

Margaret Jamison's highly visible personal style and engaging personality made her popular with collectors and artists alike and contributed to the gallery's success. It was typical of Margaret that she went to Cerrillos in her Cadillac with her driver and took Douglas Johnson to dinner. They liked one another immediately, and he started showing his work at the Jamison Gallery. His paintings sold as fast as he could create them and attracted new collectors who consistently purchased his works.

Chaco Doorways, casein on paper, 14" x 12", 1971

Tano Bowl, casein on paper, 14″ x 12″, 1970

Douglas won second prize in the 1973 New Mexico Fine Arts Biennial at the Fine Arts Museum in Santa Fe with a painting appropriately titled *Santa Fe Train Passing Through the Land of Enchantment.* Along with mandalas and landscapes with trains, he was doing paintings based on mystical aspects of the Indian world. In one, a number of people atop a mesa are lifting ladders to the clouds, an obvious recollection of the stories he had heard on the Navajo Reservation.

Much that has been written about Douglas Johnson has focused on him as a regional artist, painting American Indian subjects, but his work has grown to include many other subjects. He has produced still life paintings of birds and flowers, architectural paintings, works inspired by his travels to México, Perú, and the Orient, as well as paintings which combine a number of disparate elements in a surreal and intriguing collage format.

It has been said that art is not a hundred yard dash, but rather a relay race in which one picks up the batons from the past, runs with them and then passes them along. Some of Johnson's most important sources of inspiration have included the Navajo painters he first discovered on the reservation. From the French Impressionists and German Expressionists, whose work he first learned about in San Francisco, he learned the use of highly patterned areas in landscapes and interiors, as in the work of Klimpt and Vuillard. From Japanese prints he took the idea of depicting flowers and other objects in close-up against landscape backgrounds, especially as Hokusai did in his early woodcut prints. Johnson has been particularly interested in early Italian and Dutch religious painting and calls a painting he did of Saint Sebastian a tribute to Mantegna. Other sources as disparate as Persian miniatures, Mimbres Indian designs, Mayan and Zapotec murals and glyphs, and the works of Diego Rivera have become part of the storehouse of images that fuels his inspiration.

In working with these influences, Johnson has subordinated them to his personal vision and style, using them to help create a body of work that is unique. Collectors want paintings for their walls that intrigue and enchant them, and Douglas Johnson's paintings are forever interesting to look at. His work has steadily changed and developed through the years, reflecting the growth of his vision and an increasing integration of his life and art.

NOTES

1. Robert Ewing, *Eight from Santa Fe* (Santa Fe: Museum of New Mexico, 1970), 2.
2. Ibid., 5.
3. Virginia Kirby, *The New Mexican,* 13 December 1970, D2.

People at Rainbow's End, pencil on matboard, 8 1/2" x 14", 1975

Chimney Pots, casein on paper, 9" x 12", 1975

Train with Red Wheels, gouache on paper, 5 1/2" x 7", 1976

Emergence, gouache on matboard, 7″ x 9″, 1992

CHAPTER FOUR

Sanctuary at Agua Sarca

By 1973, Johnson's growing popularity and his proximity to Santa Fe were causing too many interruptions. He came to see that his work required a simple, more isolated lifestyle without so many distractions. He had stopped using hallucinogenics, which he realized were not conducive to maintaining the kind of rigorous schedule he needed for his painting, but the other problems remained and he longed for the solitude he had known on the Navajo reservation.

He went to see some land a friend owned in a remote area of the Jémez Mountains. Despite the extreme isolation and severity of the area, he felt that he had come home when he saw the staggering beauty of the place under a fresh January snowfall. He was able to trade his house and land in Cerrillos for the land in the Jémez, an area called Agua Sarca, and his father gave him a pickup truck to make it possible for him to live there. It took courage to leave Cerrillos and the success and relative comfort he had found there, but he felt a deep urge to retreat to a simpler, less accessible place.

At first in Agua Sarca he camped in the shelter of an overhanging rock while he observed the land and planned what he would do. He remembers:

When I first came to Agua Sarca in August of 1973, I was terrified. Not only was the place at a higher elevation with a different landscape than what I had been accustomed to on the reservation and Cerrillos, it seemed vastly empty on my first encounter. I had planned to return to Cerrillos for the winter, but the summer and fall were so gorgeous in this new place I could not leave. Not only

was there a creek with waterfalls and bathing pools, but thousands of wild flowers, lush grassland, dense forest and cliffs with suitable ledges for building. An old Hispanic adobe ruin stood on top of a level cliff and directly below it was an overhang of rock that soon became a living space once cleared of rubble. Within weeks I began building a cliff house in front of the overhang with stone and adobes harvested from a nearby ruin. Though tiny, the new house with magnificent views of mesa and canyon became so comfortable by autumn, I knew I could never return to Cerrillos for the winter. That autumn was the most magical I had ever known. The thousands of oaks in Agua Sarca turned to a spectrum of colors from red to orange to gold. Snow came early and stayed on the ground longer. The new climate was colder and wetter than I had known elsewhere, but I knew that I had found the proper place to live and continue to develop my work.[1]

Johnson continued painting, although his living and working conditions were very primitive. Had not the years on the Navajo Reservation taught him how to live with the land, he believes he could not have survived. He first built a new stone and adobe structure under the rock overhang, doing all the work himself. This house, which was entered by a ladder, gave Johnson the feeling of living as early man had lived centuries before. The small space and the style of building he emulated influenced his art. He was soon working in a smaller size that evolved into the perfect format for his carefully composed, highly detailed work. He writes:

I began scaling down landscapes, buildings, images when very young while setting up my model trains and building miniature

47

The upper story windows of Douglas Johnson's cliff-dwelling

worlds they ran through. Later, on the Navajo reservation I explored the ancient cliff dwellings of the Anasazi. Due to the size of the early Indians, rather small people by today's standards, the living spaces and villages themselves were on a smaller scale. Whole towns were tucked away in caves fitted into rock shelves and overhangs. When I began building into the cliffside at Agua Sarca, my buildings assumed the same size, small spaces, small windows, low doorways, scaled down to fit the cliffside, economical to heat and maintain. Naturally the paintings became small also, as my world became scaled down, economical.

During the first winter in Agua Sarca the *Santa Fean Magazine* published an article that drew attention to Johnson's isolated home and lifestyle, setting the tone for many of the interviews and articles written about the artist in the following years. The cover of the magazine reproduced one of his drawings in black, white, and terra cotta. The drawing was an extension of his mandalas, with the profusion of symbolic designs placed against open areas which enhanced them like a mat surrounding a painting. The article, written by Marion Love, began: "Douglas Johnson is a young, exuberant painter of crisp Southwestern themes which combine the real with the abstract."[2] A brief biographical sketch was followed by a description of his new home and his lifestyle:

Douglas left Cerrillos for a more reclusive spot and now lives and works in a handsome cliff dwelling high on the side of a remote and silent canyon. Inspired by the cliff dwellings he had found so thrilling in the great canyons of Arizona, Douglas built his rock and adobe room in classic adobe style to suit what he calls his "13th century illusion." The room is set upon bedrock which thrusts out from a shallow cave formed by a cliff overhang. Douglas leveled the rock shelf by laying flat stone and cobble in cement. Between the stones he set gleaming bits of obsidian, shells and pieces of ancient decorated black-on-white Pueblo pottery. A heavy beam set across

the cave mouth supports his roof of stripped spruce poles and willows. The roof slopes upward and out above narrow glass window panes. . . . Douglas leans his four-pole easel against the heavy beam and seats himself before it to paint, much in the manner of the old Navajo woman before her loom. He paints and draws, makes his pottery and smiles in triumph at the way he lives in beauty. However, he does admit, looking out upon his wilderness, "It's a good thing I'm young."[3]

Johnson continued to produce pottery by traditional Indian methods, the rudiments of which he had learned from the Navajo, and the more advanced techniques from Lupe Montoya at Santo Domingo Pueblo. He carefully selects natural clay and adds fine sand from dunes near Canyon del Muerto, to minimize shrinking and cracking. After the clay has been prepared, he rolls it into coils which he pinches together and shapes into dishes, pots, cups, and mugs. When the pieces are leather hard, he polishes them with smooth stones before applying designs in a natural paint made from *guaco* or Rocky Mountain Bee Plant, or colored clay slips mixed with water to the consistency of cream. He decorates each piece with his original designs. The most difficult part of the process is the firing, which he had to learn by trial and error after watching the procedure in the Pueblos. A pit is dug and a fire of clean-burning cedar is laid in it. The pottery pieces are placed on iron grills above the fire and covered with potsherds, cow dung, and more cedar. The firing takes at least four hours and often pieces crack, but the unbroken pottery possesses a special beauty.

Douglas studied his land very carefully, and in 1974 he built the first room of what would be his home and studio "in the place where the snow melted first in the spring." The habitation was built against a massive rock, which is like a great sculpture, and forms one wall of this structure. Johnson drew inspiration from the rock work at Chaco

Magpies, gouache on paper, 7 1/8"x 8", 1989

Canyon and Mesa Verde and employed methods and materials in keeping with ancient architectural design and the site on which his own structure was built:

I learned how to lay rock in Cerrillos from an Hispano living there, but by the time I came to Agua Sarca I had studied the delicate mosaic-like rock work of Chaco Canyon and the more cut-block style of Mesa Verde. I knew that these methods depended a lot on the particular rock available in each vicinity. The rock in Agua Sarca was sandstone yet differently stratified and harder. Also I had volcanic basalt and smoothened river cobbles available from Abiquiú. Using a combination of these local rock types and with the techniques of Chaco and Mesa Verde available, over the years I constructed a two-story Pueblo style house. Doorways, lintels, vigas in pairs, window sills, flagstone floors and outdoor terracing all were derived from ancient architecture. Using only hand tools made construction very difficult, and all the leveling and terracing was done with shovels. The water to make cement was hauled in barrels and carried in buckets to the site. Stone came directly from the site, from the cliff itself, but sand was hauled in from Abiquiú. Vigas and aspen latillas were cut in the nearby mountains and brought down by truck to be lowered over the cliff to rest on the walls. Dirt for the thick, flat roofs was carried bucket by bucket to be packed over the bark and straw on top of the latillas. The intention was to build a perfectly organic home of all-natural materials as though I had taken the cliff itself and pulled it around myself like a blanket to provide shelter from the elements.[4]

At first Johnson had little contact with the handsome, proud people who lived around him. In the beginning, he lived a very solitary life in the midst of his widely scattered Hispanic neighbors. The people of northern New Mexico are understandably wary of outsiders moving in and occupying land which had belonged to local families for many generations. Tensions have been exacerbated by outsiders' exploitation of these people and by their indifference to the

Douglas Johnson sitting on the rock ledge that forms the back wall of his bedroom, 1992

Hispanic culture, which they considered to be inferior.

Needing assistance with the larger structures Johnson was building, he hired local men to help him. Friendships developed and he began to take an active interest in the local culture, which was to become another major inspiration for his paintings. He has always had a facility with languages and soon was speaking passable Spanish, which was appreciated by the Hispanic people, who still prefer their native language to English. Today Douglas is fluent in Spanish and actively participates in the life of his community. He is, in fact, something of a local celebrity. The town of Española, where he shops and obtains services, lies about forty-five minutes away and he is recognized there as "the artist from Coyote."

Northern New Mexico has a distinct art tradition of its own which Johnson greatly appreciates and enjoys. It ranges from the "low-rider" automobiles, custom painted with elaborate finishes, to hand-carved *santos*, holy figures which have been made in the region for centuries, and blankets and other weavings in colorful traditional designs, usually woven with hand-dyed local wools. He admires the people

51

Top of the Stalk, gouache on paper, 8" x 5 7/8", 1987

who, like the Navajo, are fine-looking, proud and resourceful, and able to make a living under adverse conditions.

In 1975 Johnson had his first one-man show at the Jamison Gallery in Santa Fe. Margaret Jamison recognized that it would be important for his career to have an exhibition, but Johnson also needed a steady income while preparing the show. Allen Harrill, the assistant director of the gallery, introduced him to a collector from Florida named Robert Feldman, who agreed to pay Johnson a monthly stipend so that he could complete a sufficient number of paintings for the exhibition.

For the first time it was possible to see a room filled with Johnson's paintings. In the catalogue for the exhibition Feldman wrote:

If a label must be attached to Douglas's work, it could be called Indian Mysticism. In a larger sense the enduring intrinsic quality of his art remains extant over boundless time. The statement Johnson simply makes is that the primacy of nature is self-evident and some aboriginal people appreciating this vital force created a varied cultural permanency which persists through history. The colors of the land, earth's rich brown and reds, the muted blues and greens of the sky and trees, Douglas Johnson painstakingly portrays on his board with exacting detail. His singular style reflects the way in which he lives, the way he thinks and the way he feels about himself.[5]

The photograph of Johnson in that catalogue became something of an icon. He is shown without a shirt, sitting in front of one of his rock walls with an expression that is both serene and far seeing.

Johnson built the second room of his home in 1976 and added five more acres to his land. During this period he traveled extensively in the Four Corners Area and met more Pueblo people such as Anthony Lowden, son of Lucey Lowden, a well-known weaver and doll maker from Jémez Pueblo. One of his good Hispanic friends, Rudy Bendiola, was killed at age sixteen in an automobile accident. Johnson did a very moving painting of Rudy, showing him lying in state with his spirit transformed into a kachina, a spirit being, ascending into the heavens. Thereafter, Johnson began adding more human figures to his paintings.

Marion Love revisited Douglas Johnson in Agua Sarca in 1977 and in another article in the *Santa Fean Magazine* described the progress he had made since that first winter in building his home.

Douglas used to live in a smaller cliff dwelling which he fashioned for himself, but he lived there only a short time while he looked around for the warmest cliff face on his fifteen acres of property. He found a superb one in the north cliff of the canyon. . . . Right above the new home is a twelve foot long petroglyph of a snake pecked into the cliff. The snake is an Indian water symbol, and Douglas believes this one refers to the grassy, willowy marsh below his house which swarms with little water snakes. The cliff also bears inscriptions of Spanish names and glyphs of horses. Besides the water serpent, there are shards of broken pottery up and down the canyon, and many smoke stained rock shelters, all attesting to the Indians who camped and hunted there through the centuries. . . .

A Pueblo style ladder reaches up from the ground floor through a T-shaped opening into the bedroom and studio, where Douglas banded the stonework in classic Chaco Canyon style. . . . The back wall "sculptured into fantastic shapes by wind and rain" has natural niches in it where Douglas has planted mosses and ferns. . . . His tall easel of cedar and its supports rest on the white flagstone floor and against the vigas. He sits cross-legged on the floor in front of it to paint. His deeply set corner windows, patterned after some in the ruins of Chaco Canyon, let in plenty of light and a view of forested mountains and mesas.

At night, the house is lit by kerosene lamps and the aspen poles in the ceilings and in the little windows glow with a golden light.

In spite of the harsh environment and the tons of firewood Douglas must cut to heat his two rooms, he has made a world of

Front view of Douglas Johnson's cliff dwelling

beauty and comfort. "I don't want to impose it on anyone else, but I've been trying to come up with a satisfying life for myself, and this seems to be it." [6]

Johnson began showing his work at the Return Gallery in Taos, just off the main plaza. He helped design the gallery, which incorporated elements of Chaco Canyon architecture similar to those in his home and studio. In 1977 he had a second one-man show at the Jamison Gallery titled *Obsidian Mountain*, which included lithographs and drawings as well as paintings. George McKee, one of his collectors, wrote in the catalogue:

[Johnson's] ambition is said to be an envisioning of the experience of a twelfth-century Pueblo muralist. Be that as it may, the idea suggests a parallel to Douglas' great care in the formulation of his subjects and their immaculate execution; one recalls a construct of Pueblo ceremonialism to address with all dignity the powers of nature in order that they maintain their traditional comings and going on earth. [7]

The curator of Fine Arts of the Museum of Modern Art in Paris, Suzanne Page, attended the show. Her comments point up a distinctive feature of Johnson's work:

Certainly Johnson is an admirable example of an artist who has developed a unique style of his own and who has perfected a rather amazing technique for presenting his statements.

The aspect of his works which intrigues me is the aura of surrealism. I say "aura" because not always are surrealistic elements present. They only seem to be. To be sure, in some of his paintings there is an object or two in a setting unnatural to it, but in most cases there is nothing more unreal about his paintings than his own enchanted technique which is aided perhaps at times by a close up view of pottery or corn or other item in the foreground as if the painting were based on the view often taken by a wide angle camera lens when both foreground and background are in sharp perspective. [8]

In 1977 Robert Feldman encouraged Johnson to move to the Elaine Horwitch Gallery in Santa Fe, a move that would give him an opportunity to show with other contemporary southwestern artists. Elaine Horwitch had organized what was considered to be one of the best galleries in Santa Fe. A dynamic person who already had another successful gallery in Scottsdale, Arizona, Horwitch had assembled an outstanding stable of artists, including Fritz Scholder, and had made her gallery an important element of the Santa Fe art scene. By showing his work with Horwitch, Douglas Johnson was also able to exhibit in her Scottsdale gallery. By now, he was attracting many notable collectors, such as James DeVries from Michigan, Santa Feans Peter Goodwin, Letta Wofford, and Robert Love, who became a friend and mentor as well as an important financial advisor.

His first exhibition at the Horwitch Gallery was a two-person show with abstract painter Frank Ettenberg. One critic writing of the exhibition tried to describe, as others had

Orioles, gouache on paper, 7" x 13", 1989

before him, what it is that makes Johnson's work unique:

Johnson's paintings are most intriguing for their compact, highly detailed and immaculately rendered precision. Far from the realm of photo-realism, or, for that matter, from any popular contemporary realist style, Johnson's work nevertheless encompasses a strikingly super-real imagery, almost illustrative, which is as enchanting as the real places he depicts. This subject matter includes Indian adobe buildings on mountain tops. . . . And Spanish buildings like the church at Trampas.

In many of these pictures, Johnson has added his own version of twelfth-century Indian decorations within the architecture. Though historically inaccurate, as acknowledged by the artist, these motifs add interest to the paintings, by way of color, composition, and a subtle, thoughtful transcendence of history. . . . Johnson paints what he likes. He does it well, and his choices are not without considerable insight.[9]

Winter Blues, gouache on paper, 9 1/2" x 7 1/8", 1990

Douglas Johnson's work was a puzzle to many of the people who wrote about him because it did not fit in any category of art. His work was unique, neither abstract, realist, nor surreal in the accepted sense of those terms. Viewers were enthusiastic about the paintings, finding them provocative and intriguing.

Dr. Rudolph Kieve, a psychoanalyst and art collector with a very pronounced taste for the avant garde, wrote a review that was rather acerbic in tone and offered a puzzling mixture of art criticism and attributions of psychopathology. Kieve wrote:

If you accept the standards and premises Douglas Johnson sets for himself in his work, you come to accept him as a minor master of miniature painting. If, on the other hand, you question them and break him out of his hermetic limitations and try to place him somewhere in the context of contemporary visual arts, you discover that there is no room for him whatsoever. . . . He is a hermit living in a

Hummingbirds, gouache on paper, 7 7/8″ x 8 1/2″, 1989

The Martyrdom of St. Sebastian, casein on paper, 8 1/8" x 6 1/8", 1989

combination of fortress, tomb and look-out, literally and spiritually in the center of a bewitched territory, where he reigns supreme and solo as chief warlock, practicing his complex rites that are to keep him safely in a permanent state of self-hypnosis. . . . Some absolute conviction about some unknowable certainty inside the artist's heart . . . makes Johnson's work remarkable. Take it or leave it, but go and see it.[10]

In contrast, Jungian analyst Joan Buresch opens the door to personal response, allowing herself to enter Johnson's world and engage it impressionistically.

The Johnson paintings I have seen, completed between 1985 and 1995, challenge fixed systems of imagining space and time, vertical and horizontal, large and small, inside and outside, past and present, personal and impersonal. These paintings are structured around archetypal images that send one on inner journeys that circumambulate a variety of meanings. This can happen whether one likes the images or not.

Johnson's paintings, miniature in size and of beauty and precision, raise expectations of timeless moments caught and preserved for endless delight, such as we find in Persian miniatures. I, however, discover something quite different and no less rewarding. Strolling through the collection, I am first stopped by the painting of lovely young indigenous women picking berries, half-hidden in plump yellow-green bushes [see opposite page]. *They appear to have been picking berries forever. But I experience it not as a moment suspended in time, but a dynamic time-space continuum without recognizable end. How long then is endless? In my imagination, heated by this dilemma of the senses, the young women kaleidoscope from young to old and back again . . . until, hanging in timelessness I question their very existence. Staring at the image the thought arises, form and formlessness are two sides of one coin.*

Across the room is a painting of St. Sebastian. He stands handsome, oversized, with a beautiful, restrained, and most worthy Christian halo, a Native American face, painted, a pueblo dance

Harvesting Rosehips, gouache on matboard, 5" x 7 1/2", 1993

Stellar Ceremonial, gouache on paper, 8 1/4" x 8 1/8", 1985

Church at Las Trampas, Christmas Eve Procession, gouache on matboard, 7" x 8 3/4", 1996

skirt, and a body pierced with arrows, He is surrounded with historical paraphernalia: Spanish soldiers, priest(s), nuns, church, and, moving into the background in stages, the appealing architecture of ancient times. What is affecting is that the more I look, the more his imposing but impersonal body appears to be the very pillar of the foreground building. Whether this is true in painted fact is left ambiguous, but no matter, for by this time this individual historical saint has "become" the suffering world and I have come to the startling recognition that suffering is, indeed, one of the solid pillars of life. It is one thing we can be assured of, and yet . . . in a doorway nearby, tiny Native American sacred clowns are playing impishly,

enacting our absolute birthright to joy and laughter and highlighting the truth that joy is only a heartbeat away from suffering.

There is no doubt a sister/brotherhood of those who wish to be tossed about on the horns of existential dilemmas such as I describe arising from a viewing of Johnson's paintings. The poet Keats speaks to this, describing what he calls admiringly "negative capability" . . . that is "when man is capable of being in uncertainties, mysteries, doubts, without any irritable reaching after fact or reason." For those who by delight or absolute necessity are drawn to the complexity of things, there is much to find in the work of Douglas Johnson."

61

San Estevan de Ácoma, gouache on matboard, 6" x 9 7/8", 1996

NOTES

1. Douglas Johnson, interview with the author, winter 1996.

2. Marion Love, "Douglas Johnson: It's a Good Thing I'm Young," *The Santa Fean,* February-March 1974, 12.

3. Ibid., 13.

4. Douglas Johnson, interview with the author, winter 1996.

5. Robert Feldman, *Douglas Johnson* (Santa Fe: Jamison Gallery, June 1975), 2.

6. Marion Love, "Douglas Johnson, Painter-Builder, 13th Century Man," *The Santa Fean,* July 1977, 11-13.

7. George McKee. *Obsidian Mountain,* (Santa Fe: Jamison Gallery, July 1977), 3.

8. The *Santa Fe New Mexican,* 27 July 1975.

9. Walter Lonlak, "Gallery Critique," *The Santa Fe Reporter,* 2 September, 1978.

10. Rudolph Kieve, "Ettenberg: Living up to Expectations," *The Santa Fe New Mexican,* 21 September 1978.

11. Joan Buresch, review, 1997.

Masks, gouache on paper, 5 3/8" x 6 3/8", 1985

Mockingbirds, gouache on paper, 6 3/4" x 7 1/4", 1989

Brothers of Light, gouache on matboard, 6 1/2" x 8 7/8", 1990

San Carlos Borromeo, Mission Carmel, gouache on matboard, 8 1/2″ x 9 1/2, 1997

Nuestra Señora de los Chiles, gouache on matboard, 9" x 5", 1992

Maguey, gouache on paper, 8" x 8", 1980

CHAPTER FIVE

A Wider World: The Odyssey Continues

In 1978, traveling to México for the first time, Johnson came in contact with a whole new world of inspiration. His work continued to incorporate more human figures than before, and he found the striking looking people of México to be interesting subjects who were congenial to his themes and style. The archaeological ruins and the exotic country itself stimulated his imagination and were to have a lasting impact on his paintings. On the first trip of two weeks, he spent time on the Pacific Coast and the Central Plateau where he visited the site of the ancient city of Teotihuacán with its extraordinary pyramids. In 1979 he returned to México, spending six weeks in Oaxaca, where he visited the ruins of Mitla and Monte Albán. For the first time he began to paint flowers, using the compositional device he had loved in the work of Hokusai, of placing a large flower in the foreground, but using a background of jungle or pre-Columbian ruins.

In the fall of 1979, Johnson's joint exhibition with jeweler John Hernández of Taos at the Museum of New Mexico, and later at the Colorado Springs Fine Arts Center, reflected these new themes and treatments. In the Santa Fe *New Mexican*, Rosanna Hall wrote of his paintings of this period:

Johnson's miniature paintings done in casein during a visit to Oaxaca, México are a mysterious blend of Central American, Mesoamerican, and New Mexico Pueblo Indian cultures. Each painting is a tiny, detailed world of temples approached by adobe brick stairways, prickly cactus and flowers, tombstones, pillars and starry skies.

In combining cultures which flourished before Western man arrived in the New World, Johnson has managed to visually tell how the ritual and formal world looked in the all-Indian cultures. Whether the New World really was as colorful and orderly as Johnson says it was, he has at least created a world of his own that is a joy to look over his shoulder to see.

Johnson's incredible ability to capture the smallest detail of a thorn on a cactus, or the shadow of a stone is blended beautifully with his feeling for space in eternity.[1]

México also opened a new world of color for Johnson; his work from then on is characterized by rich, fully saturated hues. He also began showing *tablitas*, paraphrasing the head adornment worn by Pueblo women in their ceremonial dances. To make them, he cut geometric shapes out of mat board and painted them much as he had his mandalas, often ornamenting them with feathers and beads.

The year 1979 brought successes for Johnson, but also personal tragedy. His grandmother died in the autumn, and his mother died on Christmas Eve of the same year. The following August further tragedy struck with the death of his sister Claudia from complications of anorexia. Fortunately, he had maintained a close relationship with his father, who managed to come to most of the openings for Johnson's exhibitions.

In 1981 Johnson was commissioned to do the annual poster for the Santa Fe Opera, a coveted and prestigious honor in the Santa Fe art community. The subject he chose was the altar screen, or *reredo*, in the Saint Francis Cathedral in Santa Fe. His choice of an important New Mexican

69

Flor de Oaxaca, gouache on paper, 9 1/4" x 6", 1979

subject rather than something relating to the opera was well received and opened a new source of inspiration for him, as he was increasingly drawn to the local Hispanic culture for subject matter in his paintings.

Johnson traveled to México again in 1981, spending three months in Huayapan, a Zapotec village near Oaxaca, where he continued his series of paintings of flowers and archaeological ruins. In a subsequent interview Johnson was asked if he painted different subjects in México, and he answered:

[In New Mexico] I paint Chaco Canyon, and down there I paint Monte Albán. They're very similar. When I first went to Teotihuacán, I had the strangest feeling. When I first walked onto that main avenue there, I felt "This is Chaco Canyon!" and it's a whole different culture. I don't understand it. It's just a feeling I have. When I go to Chaco now I think of Teotihuacán.[2]

In Huayapan Johnson felt that his Mexican paintings had matured and he was painting better than ever before. He describes his experiences during this period:

I began traveling to México during the coldest and darkest days of the New Mexico winter. Not only did México give me a warm relief from winter, but it gave me new subjects to paint and newer, brighter colors. The many shades of the bougainvillea, the sensuous tropical pinks, oranges and reds brightened my palette tremendously. Several winters living among the Zapotec Indians of Huayapan, seeing this experience through the eyes of Diego Rivera, gave me new insights into painting. The Zapotecs lived a life similar to the ancient Anasazi of the American Southwest. Women still spent hours grinding corn on metates, lived and slept on woven floor mats in small adobe houses with large extended families, and traded at big colorful markets in village plazas. They still used hand-crafted pottery and carried water in large pottery jars on their heads. They still wove their own clothing and even used a head strap to carry large loads on their backs.

Mixtec Palace, Mitla, gouache on paper, 5 1/2" x 11", 1982

Breaking Earth, Pisac, Perú, gouache on paper, 4 1/2" x 7 1/4", 1983

I rented a one-room adobe house in the village of Huayapan and befriended a family that fed and protected me. Although they spoke Zapotec, I learned Oaxacan Spanish from them—no one spoke English this far south in México. I still retain this dialect of Spanish, which is very different from that spoken in northern New Mexico. I set up my easel and in the cool shade of my house in Huayapan, surrounded by coffee bushes and avocado trees, I painted the Zapotecs of the present and their ancestors in pre-Columbian times in the settings of Monte Albán, Mitla and Yagul. Evenings I spent in the city of Oaxaca, where I made many friends who took me on journeys throughout Oaxaca and Chiapas, experiencing first hand the rich culture of southern México.[3]

Johnson visited Huayapan again in 1982, but this time was caught up in trouble between feuding families, which made it impossible for him to return to the village.

On his return to the United States, he visited James DeVries in Michigan. The DeVries collection, which contained almost sixty of Johnson's paintings and most of his Mexican works, was being shown at the Krasl Art Center. That year he also had exhibits in Lincoln, Nebraska, and in Corpus Christi, Texas as well as in Santa Fe and Taos.

A critic wrote of the Taos exhibition: "Douglas Johnson creates a small, patterned, still, but utterly compelling world of scenes from pre-Columbian life. His figures standing in fields of giant ears of corn, or watching a moonrise… have a mythic quality that is unforgettable."[4] Johnson had added a new subject, Egypt, to his paintings and often combined Egyptian and southwestern themes in startling eye-catching combinations.

In 1983, Johnson journeyed to Perú, visiting Lima and Cuzco, traveling by train from Machu Picchu across the

Andes to Lake Titicaca and on down to the Pacific Ocean. He was beguiled by the land and the people and by the archaeological ruins of the Inca. Some of his paintings reflect the political situation of the period, showing soldiers in the street in front of handsome colonial buildings. But most of the paintings are of the simple people of the Andes, their markets and everyday life, and the immense and compelling Inca ruins. He exhibited the Peruvian paintings in Santa Fe and Taos, deriving the exhibition title from three subjects: Aztlán (mythological paintings of New Mexico), Egypt, and Perú. He sometimes combined the three subjects in a startling and surprising single work.

In writing about the exhibition "Aztlán, Egypt and Perú" at Return Gallery in Taos, David Hopper describes the mystical sources of Johnson's inspiration and captures the impact of his paintings on viewers:

> Douglas Johnson creates tiny paintings that immediately depict vast scenes and cosmologies. The paintings affect us very strongly. They are crystal lattices to infinity fixed by spiritual paths of consciousness. We are projected into other dimensions of time, where reality is beautiful and sacred; where man is in rhythm with radiant nature. Johnson's way of life here in Aztlán, his winters in Oaxaca, his recent travels in Perú, his dreams of ancient Egypt, inspire the works, and the connective fibres of a common mystical basis are masterfully interwoven. . . . It is in awe that we present another definitive exhibition of the life and work of Douglas Johnson.[5]

Writing about a two-person show at Horwitch Gallery in Santa Fe which paired Douglas with Joe Baker, Suzanne Deats comments on some of the aesthetic and thematic juxtapositions that make Johnson's work distinctive:

> Johnson's small casein paintings are absolutely still, and their relentlessness derives from a fanatic attention to detail. A good many of his subjects are Central American buildings and people, all with impeccably observed architectural and costume details.

Macaws, gouache on paper, 14" x 8", 1991

Still Life with Tulips in Chinese Cup, gouache on paper, 5" x 6 1/4", 1990

For all of the authenticity, however, his works have a timeless "transcultural" quality, a ritualistic aspect common to a great many groups through the ages. So an Egyptian piece, called "The Step Pyramid of Zoser", bears a striking kinship to a painting of some South American Indians walking down an ancient street with modern graffiti on the walls. . . .

The most interesting piece in the exhibit is "The Dictator's Limousine" (see right), with a black Cadillac tail fin set against a Central American city street featuring a crowd of guerrillas rushing by. Not only does it have more political content than usual, but it is instantly memorable as a simple, classic composition. A more coherent image would be hard to find.[6]

In 1984 Johnson returned to Perú, spending time in Puno on Lake Titicaca. He found himself stranded there because of railroad strikes and unceasing rainfall. The time was not wasted, however. Johnson writes:

Waiting to find a way out of Puno, I attended the celebrations for the Virgin of the Candelaria. All day and night groups of Indian dancers, dressed as hideous serpent-haired devils, ridiculing the Spaniards, their oppressors, danced through the streets of Puno. One day, I took a boat out onto Lake Titicaca to visit the island of Taquili, an Indian stronghold untouched by modern Peruvian culture. The boatmen, who were dressed in western clothes when we left Puno, stopped to change to traditional Indian attire before reaching Taquili and changed back to western dress on the return trip.

Johnson would later do a series of paintings drawn from his experiences in Puno. He finally got to Cuzco and eventually Lima, and though the experience was not as pleasant as the year before, he amassed a collection of antique textiles and continued his series of Peruvian paintings.

When he returned to New Mexico, Johnson exhibited a second group of Peruvian paintings in Santa Fe and continued his exploration of Indian and Hispanic themes. He also continued work on his property, converting the adobe ruin

The Dictator's Limousine, Lima, Perú, gouache on paper, 6 1/2 x 6 1/8, 1984

into a studio. The adobe building proved much easier to heat than his rock house and permitted him to paint more comfortably in the winter. Johnson worked on further additions and remodeling in the next few years.

He took his longest trip in 1985, traveling to Thailand for an extended stay in northern Chang Mai and two weeks in Bangkok. He was deeply attracted to Thai Buddhism as practiced by the people and reflected in their character and lives. They were friendly and respectful and seemed very happy. The architecture of the temple compounds was like nothing he had ever experienced, with tiered, tiled roofs, walls of mosaic made from colored mirrors, golden stupas, sculptures of Buddha as well as Hindu gods and goddesses, and Chinese style gardens with lotus pools. In Thailand he collected wood carvings and porcelains and made drawings for a series of paintings.

In Santa Fe Johnson exhibited new works based on his travels and had an exhibition at Gump's in San Francisco. He was happy to take Bruno Loewenberg, then ninety-three, the man who had been his mentor many years before, to see the exhibition.

In Agua Sarca he met a young local man, Joseph Aragón, in whom he recognized a great deal of potential. With Johnson's encouragement Aragón attended Highlands University in Las Vegas, New Mexico, eventually receiving a bachelor's degree in Spanish and History. Aragón began helping Johnson with the increasingly difficult job of main-

called "Pueblo Nouveau" (see below). Completed in 1986, it is a summation of many of the themes on which he has focused throughout his career. Composed with Johnson's characteristic richness of detail, the mural celebrates the Jémez Mountains and the Río Grande Valley, showing kachinas in the mountains, Indians in the valley, and spirits in the sky and earth.

In 1987 Johnson revisited the Orient, spending time in

taining the property at Agua Sarca and became a partner in the enterprise, creating a space for his own study and writing which complements Johnson's studio.

Johnson was commissioned to create a mural for the Old House Restaurant in the new Eldorado Hotel in Santa Fe, and he designed the southwestern style dado design which decorates the hallways of the hotel. For the mural Johnson painted on an eighteen-foot panel, in a style he

Bangkok and Burma. He describes Burma as:

a backward country crumbling under a corrupt military dictator-ship. Rangoon, originally built by the British, was in the process of being reclaimed by the jungle. Nothing worked, hotels were full of rats, transportation barely functioned. In spite of all this, the people were wondrously at peace with themselves and lived simple reli-gious lives. The Buddhist temples, in contrast to the almost gaudy Thai temples, were elegant and simple. Their thirteenth-century murals portrayed scenes that were identical to contemporary Burmese life. Except for the remnants of British colonial culture, Burma was timeless—closed off from the western world, pristine, culturally intact.

Back in Thailand Johnson became friends with a monk who spoke English and spent many hours listening to him explain the precepts of Buddhism. Visiting temples and monasteries with this monk, Johnson was able to ask ques-

reer brought me some financial success. In Asia, observing Buddhist monks living simple, non-materialistic lives, desiring nothing but daily nutrition and the inner riches of peace of mind, reenforced a lifestyle I knew was correct for me. In the beginning, I knew this by instinct primarily and from reason as I grew older. In my years as a struggling artist, my goals were to dedicate my life to becoming a master of painting regardless of recognition and financial reward. Painting became a vehicle to peace of mind. My retreat to the isola-

Mural: *Río Grande*, acrylic on masonite, 4' x 18', 1986

tions and receive answers on Buddhist philosophy from other monks who spoke no English.

He found in Buddhist philosophy and the simplicity of the Buddhist lifestyle a confirmation of his own way of life and his values:

It was very early in life that I learned that richness was a life based on the mind and spirit, rather than a life of the body. Of course I fluctuated in and out of this over the years, especially when my ca-

tion in the mountains was to forsake the material world for solitude and an environment conducive to dedication to painting. The beauty of the natural world became my teacher and guide. I have never longed for anything else than to continue living in this manner. The lifestyle I created here was of simplicity and beauty, the rituals of survival meditations in their own right, from tending fires, to dipping in the spring for water, rites that I would greatly miss if I gave them up for the luxury of utilities.

77

Burmese Orchid, gouache on paper, 8 3/4" x 5 1/4", 1987

Also "consistency" has a lot to do with my lifestyle. Following a daily pattern over the years has been a form of discipline. Rising early, starting fires, carrying water, cleansing self and house, painting to sundown in natural light, chopping wood, walking the dogs, reading and researching by lamplight, sleeping. It is all part of a life ritual that supports my creative life. Life itself becomes a mantra.

After a final exhibition at the Horwitch Gallery, Johnson moved to the Gerald Peters Gallery in Santa Fe and exhibited in 1986 at the Peters Gallery in Dallas. He also exhibited in several group shows. He had a large one-man exhibition at the Santa Fe Peters Gallery in 1988, introducing the most impressive exhibition thus far in his career. The opening was well attended and attracted many collectors.

He traveled with Joseph Aragón to Yucatán, where he began painting the Mayan ruins. It was here that he began painting birds, which would become a major theme in his work. Johnson found a different México in Yucatán. Isolated from colonial México for centuries, it was virtually a nation unto itself. Mayan peasant culture still thrived, with language and lifestyle little changed from ancient times. Outside the cities Spanish culture was only a thin veneer. The ruins, once the jungle had been cleared from them, were far superior in style and artistic embellishment to those in central México. The Puuc style of the thirteenth century prevalent at Uxmal and the older Chichen Itza displayed delicate mosaic-like stonework depicting the Mayan pantheon of gods and spirits on building façades.

In Yucatán, exotic tropical birds filled the skies and Indians kept brilliantly colored parrots, macaws, cockatoos, and toucans as pets. Johnson had many opportunities to view these birds at close range. He had often thought of painting birds, and this trip to Yucatán provided the inspiration to begin his bird series.

Johnson's work was formally introduced into the New

Novice Monks in Procession to the Temple to be Shorn, gouache on paper, 6 1/4" x 8 1/8", 1988

York art scene in 1989, when he began showing his work at the J. N. Bartfield Gallery. He expanded his bird series in anticipation of his next major exhibition, which opened that same year at the Peters Gallery in Santa Fe and was titled "Birds of Magic and Other New Paintings." The catalogue describes the new series:

His current work includes a number of birds, magical in detail and accurate enough to satisfy the most demanding ornithologist. These paintings feature lavish backgrounds, ranging from jungle-bound pre-Columbian ruins to an everyday scene depicting the re-plastering of his adobe studio by a northern New Mexico family. . . . In several recent works, Johnson has selected a horizontal rectangular space which he first divides with a beautiful line. He then adds splendidly unrelated things which happen to intrigue him at the moment. In one painting a vase of flowers, a section of celestial sky, and a kachina-like figure riding on a blackbird are part of a composition, much like a collage.

Johnson's work was becoming more widely known by

79

Uxmal, gouache on paper, 7" x 6 1/4", 1988

Nasturtiums, gouache on paper, 6 3/8″ x 8 9/16″, 1989

1991. In that year a one-man show opened at the Frumpkin Gallery in Los Angeles. He was selected to paint a four-by-eight foot mural for the New Mexico State Capitol, but the project had to be delayed for lack of funds. He was also invited to participate in the federal Art in Embassies program. As part of the program, he sent a large tulip still life on loan to Beijing, China for two years.

Another one-man exhibition at the Peters Gallery in 1992 was entitled "Painting the Mythical." Like many other reviewers before him, Dean Balsamo of the *New Mexican* was struck by Johnson's ability to connect the worlds he painted on both the mythic and material levels:

There was a time people moved to Santa Fe and its environs not because of its style, but rather for the special qualities of the land and the life arising from it. Painter Douglas Johnson is part of that old guard. For more than twenty years he has struggled to balance his desire for what Buddhists would call "right livelihood" with the determination to maintain the purity of his personal vision. . . .

Living in a traditional way allows him to enter the world and rituals of contemporary Navajo, Zapotec and Pueblo life along with that of their twelfth-century ancestors.

He knows their world because he lives it. And that world, it appears from the hyper-realistic and surreal quality of his color and subject matter, is a world of vision.[8]

In 1993 a retrospective exhibition of Johnson's works was held at the Governor's Gallery at the New Mexico State Capitol. The exhibition included over eighty works, including paintings, lithographs, and polychrome pottery. The earliest work was the cover of Johnson's electric train timetable, painted in 1958, when he was in the seventh grade. Johnson gave a talk about his work to a large audience, and the show was favorably reviewed:

It is the fact that Johnson has been creating his miniature, orderly, and complex painted worlds for most of his life—35 years, beginning at age 12—that merits this retrospective at the Governor's Gallery. And, without a doubt, it is a show of merit. . . . His vibrant images collapse time in that they could be representations of today or 400 years ago. Johnson's content is conjured from the imagination and is archaeologically sound, but it is his painting style . . . that sets him apart—and several heads above—any other southwestern artist working in the same vein. A Douglas Johnson work is always immediately recognizable as a Johnson while remaining completely unique.

A beautifully curated show of eighty pieces by Johnson, from 1958 to the present, takes the viewer on a journey through the imagination that grows and develops over time . . . . By the time we get to the 1970 painting, Awaiting the Emergence into the Fifth World *[see page 39], Johnson's style is set. Depicting a scene at a pueblo where a group of worshippers stands on the roof of an elaborately painted adobe building with their backs turned to the painter, the image rises into a cloud-filled sky. Johnson's clouds are as trademark of his style as his pueblos, and they remain identifiably his from 1970 to the present.*

As we travel through time and around the room, we see Egyptian influences, images from journeys to Perú and Thailand, as well

Still Life with Polychrome Pot, Kachina, Prayerstick and Mug, gouache on matboard, 6" x 8 1/2", 1995

as a recurring train motif. The works become more and more so-phisticated, complicated, and iconoclastic. At the end, one feels an admiration that is coupled with a desire to see much more by this outstanding talent in the years to come.[9]

In 1993 Johnson taught art to fifth grade students in Hernández and Española under a Prime Time program, hoping to plant some of the seeds in the students that had been given to him by his most memorable teachers. Concentrating on images that would be meaningful to the students in cultural terms, Johnson created coloring sheets depicting local Hispanic icons derived from religious and folk art. The children worked with images of low-riders, the

Virgin of Guadalupe, Jesus with a crown of thorns, the Santuario de Chimayó (a famous pilgrimage site), and Indian dancers. The students were honest and open in their reactions. Johnson's purpose, besides allowing them to validate their culture through art, was to encourage them to draw on their own instincts, intuition, and experience and to explore their individuality and free artistic expression. Johnson looks on art as an ability inborn in all human beings, noting that in primitive societies everyone is adept at art or craft. Working with young students gives him an opportunity to introduce them to art before society's expectations have discouraged or distorted their creative impulses. Johnson's approach was perceived as too radical within the traditional

Urraca, gouache on matboard, 6 1/2" x 10 1/8", 1993

school setting, and he was not rehired the following semester.

Johnson had an exhibition entitled "Southwest Traditions, Modern Icons" in 1994 at the Peters Gallery, and collector Robert Redford bought many of the paintings. Johnson's father attended the opening with great difficulty following a stroke the previous year, managing to keep up his record of attending all of his son's openings.

While participating in an archaeological survey of the community of Río del Oso, Johnson was inspired to begin a new series of paintings based on the Spanish Colonial period. He also hung a large painting he titled "Hozhonzeh" in the New Mexico State Capitol to complete the commission that had been delayed.

In the summer of 1995 Johnson expanded his gallery affiliations to include the Stephen Parks Gallery in Taos, renewing his special relationship with that art center after an absence of ten years. In the fall of 1995 he hung a wall of paintings in a new gallery in Santa Monica, California, and another in Scottsdale, Arizona, and later that year, he moved his Santa Fe affiliation to Nedra Matteucci's Fenn Gallery.

Oriole with Hopi Pot, gouache on matboard, 3 3/4" x 7 1/4", 1994

The Birds, gouache on paper, 7 1/2" x 8 1/2", 1988

The Gambling Kachina, gouache on matboard, 5 3/4″ x 9 1/8″, 1995

It seems that the legend of the artist living in the far reaches of New Mexico can never be told too many times. Each year has brought a number of articles about Johnson which celebrate his home and studio, his lifestyle and his art.

Today, New Mexico is greatly changed from the place Douglas Johnson had dreamed of, and which he found in 1969, half his life ago. Where there were only a few art galleries, there are now over a hundred, and the "Santa Fe Style" is known world-wide. Driving from Santa Fe to visit Johnson in Agua Sarca today, one must first negotiate a busy four-lane highway past newly developed Indian gaming casinos, which he sees as a threat to the integrity of the ancient Pueblo Indian culture. Several of his recent paintings, titled *Gambling Kachinas*, reflect his feeling about this

intrusion into the country for which he cares so much.

Once away from the traffic and congestion, however, the country itself is still breathtaking as one passes through a land of magnificent mountains and mesas. As one drives up the valley of the Chama River, past the community of Abiquiú, the view around Ghost Ranch becomes truly extraordinary, with enormous cliffs banded in red and yellow dominating the landscape. The road crosses Abiquiú Dam with its blue lake, and beyond the flat-topped mountain called Pedernal one enters a pastoral region where adobe buildings and farm fields soften the foreground, framed by the surrounding cliffs. Beyond the village of Coyote, but before reaching the town of Cuba, is Douglas Johnson's Agua Sarca.

Santo Chevy, gouache on paper, 7" x 9 1/2", 1985

Moccasins, gouache on paper, 5 1/2" x 7 1/4", 1988

From the road one can see Johnson's studio with a Santa Fe Railroad medallion embedded in the wall, a memento collected years before in the time of his first enthusiasm for the railroads. At fifty, Douglas Johnson moves with the agility of someone half his age. His face and hands reflect the years of chopping wood, carrying water, and building with stone, but his eyes are as clear and bright as when he was first finding his way as an artist in Cerrillos.

In the several structures that comprise the compound one is struck by the sense of order and beauty characteristic of every aspect of Johnson's life. Each object in the many rooms is as carefully placed as are the elements in his meticulously composed paintings. Remembrances of the long journey that brought him to this place range from pieces of his mother's furniture to model trains tucked into niches in the rock wall. In the outhouse a floor-to-ceiling collage of photographs cut from magazines is a reminder of his boyhood room in California.

Down a steep path, one finds the spring of pure, cold water which provides for his daily needs and is part of every

Guérnica (The Gulf War), gouache on paper, 8 3/4″ x 9 1/2″, 1991

August Fourth, gouache on paper, 7 3/4" x 13 5/8", 1990

painting which Johnson sends into the world. The sky on a moonless night at Agua Sarca, far from the pollution of city lights, is filled with clouds of stars, and the Milky Way forms a luminous river in the night. It is easy to see this place as a constant source of inspiration for the artist.

Asked about his future, Johnson replied:

I sometimes have a fantasy of giving it all up and returning to Southeast Asia to become a monk and grow old in a monastery, restoring ancient temple murals. More realistically, I expect I will spend the rest of my life improving and perfecting my painting style, setting a positive example for younger artists, and working with students.[10]

Douglas Johnson is a maverick in the art world, a daringly original artist whose life and work are uniquely his own creation and who continues to build on new and seemingly inexhaustible sources of inspiration. As it has been from the beginning, his odyssey is a work in progress.

NOTES

1. Rosanna Hall, "Two Fine Art Shows Open," *The Santa Fe New Mexican,* September 1979.

2. Lisa Sherman-Wade, "Douglas Johnson: Paintings of Primitives," *Art Lines,* July 1981, 24-25.

3. Douglas Johnson, interview with the author, winter 1996.

4. Joanne Foreman, "Magar, Johnson in Personal Visions," *The Taos News,* 4 August 1983.

5. David Hopper, *Aztlán, Egypt, Perú* (Taos: Return Gallery, July 1983), 4.

6. Suzanne Deats, "Not Completely Dissimilar," *The Santa Fe New Mexican,* 1982.

7. Robert Ewing, *Douglas Johnson: Birds of Magic and Other New Paintings* (Santa Fe: The Gerald Peters Gallery, June 1990), 1-3.

8. Dean Balsamo, "Entering the Myth and Magic of Johnson's Casein Jewels," *The Santa Fe New Mexican Pasatiempo,* 21 August 1992.

9. Simone Ellis, "Douglas Johnson: A 35-Year Retrospective," *THE* magazine, November 1993.

10. Douglas Johnson, interview with the author, winter 1996.

Black Violets, gouache on matboard, 4 3/4″ x 8″, 1996

Buffalo Dancers with Flutes, gouache on matboard, 5 1/4" x 5 3/4", 1994

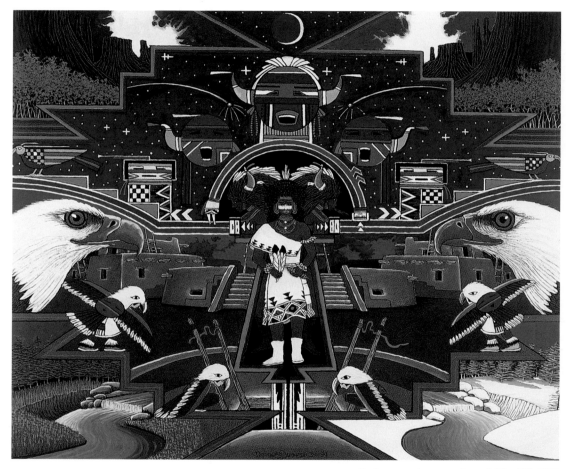

Eagles, gouache on matboard, 9" x 11", 1994

Vicente de Zaldívar, gouache on matboard, 7" x 7", 1994

Dragonfly Altar, gouache on paper, 10 3/4" x 9 7/8", 1991

Douglas Johnson: An Appreciation

MaLin Wilson

Writing about Douglas Johnson's paintings instead of his biography emphasizes their independent existence, their ability to seduce a society of their own and thereby take up far-flung residence—each on their own merits—in homes and collections across America.

Johnson has been a frequent exhibitor in Santa Fe since 1970. His solo shows always feel like a visit to a "parallel event stream"; in group exhibitions Johnson's little paintings are usually distinctively out-of-sync in the jostle of large abstractions, sweeping landscapes, minimalist grids, found objects, and figurative sculpture. Grounded in pattern and decoration, they seem so guileless, so friendly in comparison to most late twentieth-century art. Also, the extraordinary care in their construction is itself a persuasive argument for attention. They propose an ongoing acquaintance instead of a drive-by exchange. During the 1970s, three seconds was the time clocked per painting by trained observers in art galleries: In contrast, reduced scale, as in Johnson's work, actually shifts and opens time for viewers. This phenomenon has been confirmed by psychologist Alan DeLong in 1976 at the University of Tennessee. Human beings compensate for shifts in scale by increasing interaction so that something reduced to one-sixth its normal size will be processed by a factor of six. In other words, what in "real time" would be ten seconds is experienced—in terms of brain activity—as sixty. So, by walking through a gallery filled with human scale work and then being drawn toward—and into—a Douglas Johnson painting means that the beholder moves from quotidian time into another calendar. It might even be confusing coming back to the room, coming back perhaps to a gallery attendant at one's elbow who speaks an incomprehensible tongue.

Even though I have thought about it, I know that I can't just grab one of Douglas Johnson's little worlds . . . and run away with it. Galleries require at least a semblance of acceptable behavior. This bid to be taken home in arms, adopted, as it were, is essential to the exchange proposed by Johnson's works. They seek to be companions through life's passages. Like medieval illuminations, his miniatures are a northern New Mexico "Book of Hours." They are works of worship, a celebration of enduring domestic cycles of life lived in the countryside, in pueblos, and rural villages.

I have always thought of Douglas Johnson as an artist championed by his collectors, an artist whose progeny are first embraced domestically and finally recognized by museums and institutions who have felt obliged to catch up. The reasons for this are obvious, quite significant, and became more apparent during Johnson's 1993 retrospective at the Governor's Gallery in Santa Fe. Like the lapidary visual

97

Calabazas, gouache on matboard, 5 5/8" x 8 3/4", 1993

field of each painting, this retrospective was jam-packed. In the exhibition/reception area of the Governor's Gallery there were approximately seventy works on paper including juvenalia, paintings, and prints. Mostly they looked like devotional illustrated manuscripts from an oral society.

Since Johnson never attended art school his work has always operated outside the rather narrow band of academic lineage; and although dependent on the market town of Santa Fe he has not cultivated the shifting "isms" of art-speak. This means that the best an art critic can suggest in regards to looking at Johnson's work is a familiarity with a wide range of sources—Egyptian funerary art, Persian miniatures, fourteenth-century Sienese painters, William Blake, Otto Runge, heraldry, Walt Disney, "Love Generation" San Francisco album covers, and early twentieth-century Native American genre paintings by such artists as Harrison Begay and Pablita Velarde. Johnson mediates visual traditions used worldwide with a kind of 1960s adventurousness and saturated psychedelic palette. Without the prejudices of teachers and peers, he builds his lexicon from whatever visual traditions are interesting and useful to him. While there is humor, his work eschews the condition of irony that saturates late twentieth-century mainstream art. All of these attributes give Douglas Johnson's imagery an accessibility at the most basic level: It invites anyone who is interested rather than addressing art world aficionados with insider codes. This helps explain why his works are first adopted into loving homes before they become institutionalized.

Now, as to the combination of exactitude and quietude: While Johnson's paintings include both personal and culturally specific symbols, every motif on a pot, the weave of a sash, the petals on a flower, or feathers on a bird are rendered with scientific rigor, yet they are not naturalistic and never fleshily Baroque. The point of view is straight

Mesa of Flowers, gouache on paper, 6 1/2" x 6 1/2", 1991

ahead—the perspective of equals—indeed the complexity proposes that the beholder sit . . . quietly . . . and study. All is stilled herein for contemplation. This style of stillness leads the eye from one detail to the next in overall fields that claim the same significance for cloud, plant, rock, animal, and weed. These elements are consecrations of Native American and Hispanic views that do not separate the religious from the secular. There are different kinds of arcadia and Johnson's is not the shaggy, dark kind that raises solitary panic; his is filled with precise, sparkling, bucolic images of treasured cultural inheritance. The resolution and careful planning in Johnson's bright works both satisfy and tweak a certain anxiety in me, for they attest to an orderliness beyond my experience. While our media-manipulated culture programs us for quick thrills, Johnson's calm meditations testify that another template is possible. They are

99

Pink Iris, gouache on paper, 7 3/4" x 6 1/4", 1991

documents of a single soul who remained from the back-to-the-earth tidal wave of cosmopolitan American youth during the 1960s. Johnson's intense and complex images of arcadia, like Virgil's Georgics, depend upon the visual tastes of the city having a romance with the country.

Douglas Johnson's paintings are embedded with rhythms from macro to micro, from ancient generational cycles to seasonal rituals, from life's passages to the pulse of a tiny brush. Together they build a tesselated overall field, from the position of a celestial deity to the kernels of a corn cob. Stroke-by-stroke. Just as a single painting can embody many different scales from tiny jet planes to monumental grain pots, they entrain us with everything from a deep base hum to a staccato chant. Horizontal landscapes stretch out internally in layered frequencies so that they become musical scores. A single composition may include crackling clouds, with the bright lines like snow, resting on the strong beat of rock walls, and the rattle of dried grasses swept by a breeze.

Douglas Johnson's paintings take a long view and remind me of the tolerant amusement expressed by a Native American speaker at a tourism conference in Santa Fe: Tourism, yes . . . well, it had always been here. With the Europeans it had accelerated in the last four hundred years but his people were planning to be here throughout and beyond that time, attending to their ceremonial year. This said, the speaker's mobile phone rang. On his way home to a tribal meeting he would stop at the pueblo's casino; and, tomorrow there was a public dance and feast day. We were all invited.

Douglas Johnson invites and proposes another sort of exchange. Look, listen, pay attention, slow down, take your time. Connect with different rhythms. They are many. Your choice.

Nativity, after Pablita Velarde, gouache on paper, 5 5/8" x 8 1/2", 1993

1484, gouache on paper, 7 5/8" x 5 1/2", 1984

Tewa Deer Dance, gouache on paper, 5 1/2" x 7 5/8", 1990

Poshuouinge Winter, gouache on matboard, 6" x 6", 1995

Poshuouinge Spring, gouache on matboard, 6" x 6", 1995

Poshuouinge Summer, gouache on matboard, 6 1/2" x 6 1/2", 1995

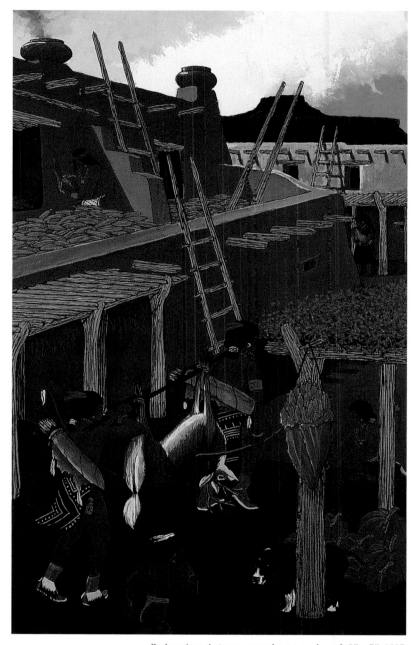

Poshuouinge Autumn, gouache on matboard, 8" x 5", 1995

Christmas, gouache on paper, 7 1/8" x 9 5/8", 1988

Return of the Kachinas, gouache on paper, 6 1/4" x 10 1/2", 1990

Descending Sacred Mountain, gouache on paper, 5" x 9", 1988

Santo Domingo Church, gouache on matboard, 6 3/4" x 8 3/4", 1995

LIST OF PLATES